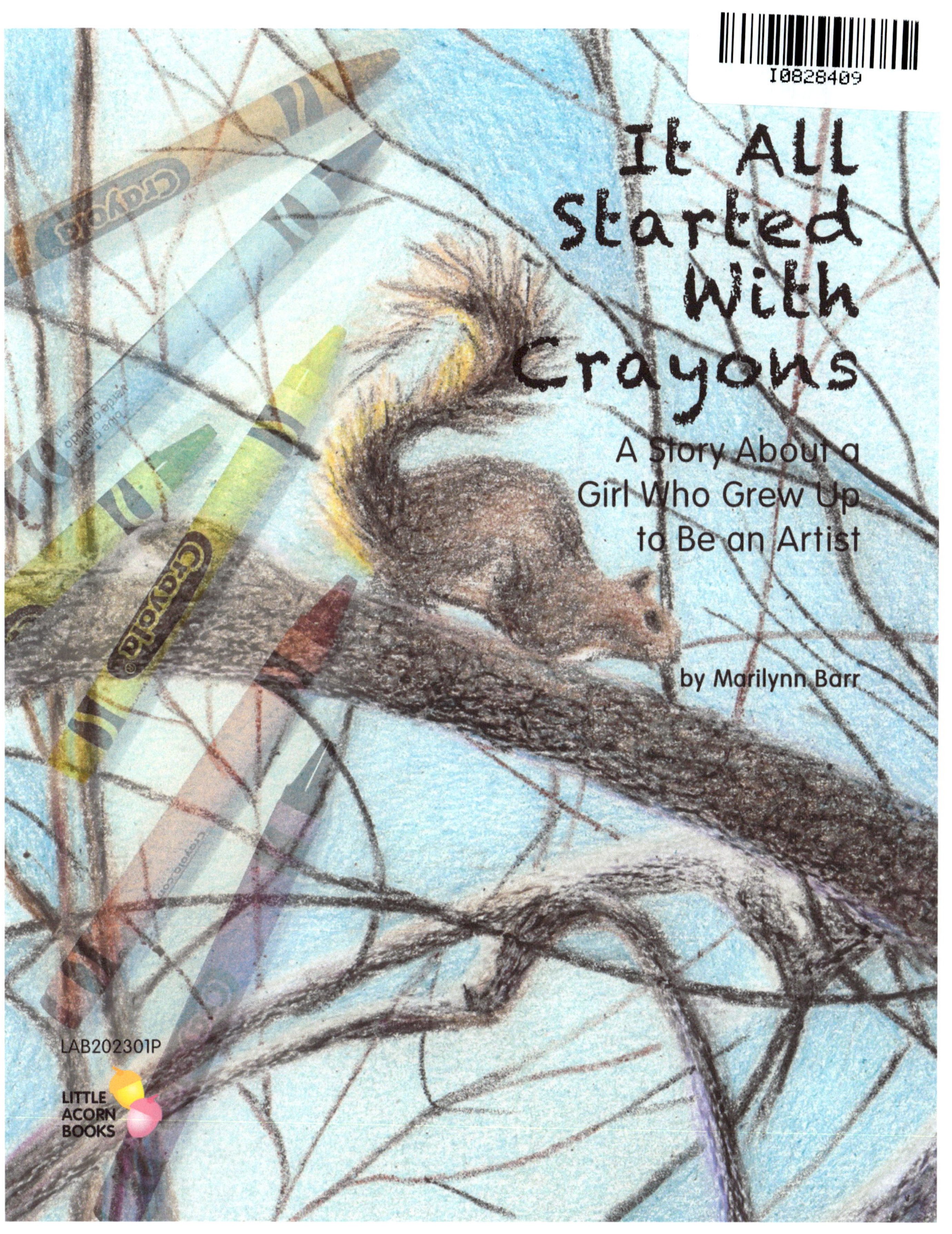

It All Started With Crayons

A Story About a Girl Who Grew Up to Be an Artist

by Marilynn Barr

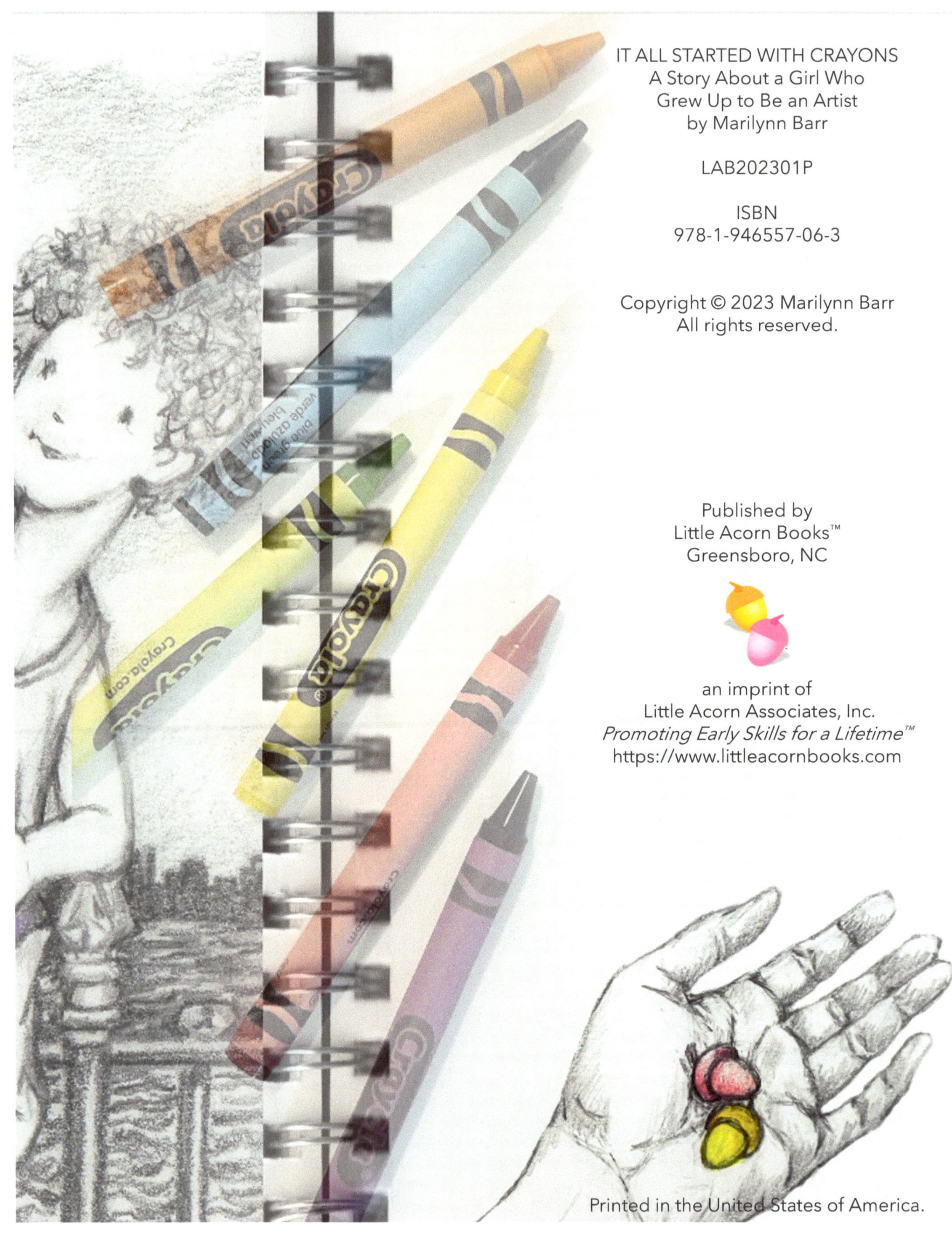

IT ALL STARTED WITH CRAYONS
A Story About a Girl Who
Grew Up to Be an Artist
by Marilynn Barr

LAB202301P

ISBN
978-1-946557-06-3

Published by
Little Acorn Books™
Greensboro, NC

an imprint of
Little Acorn Associates, Inc.
Promoting Early Skills for a Lifetime™
https://www.littleacornbooks.com

Printed in the United States of America.

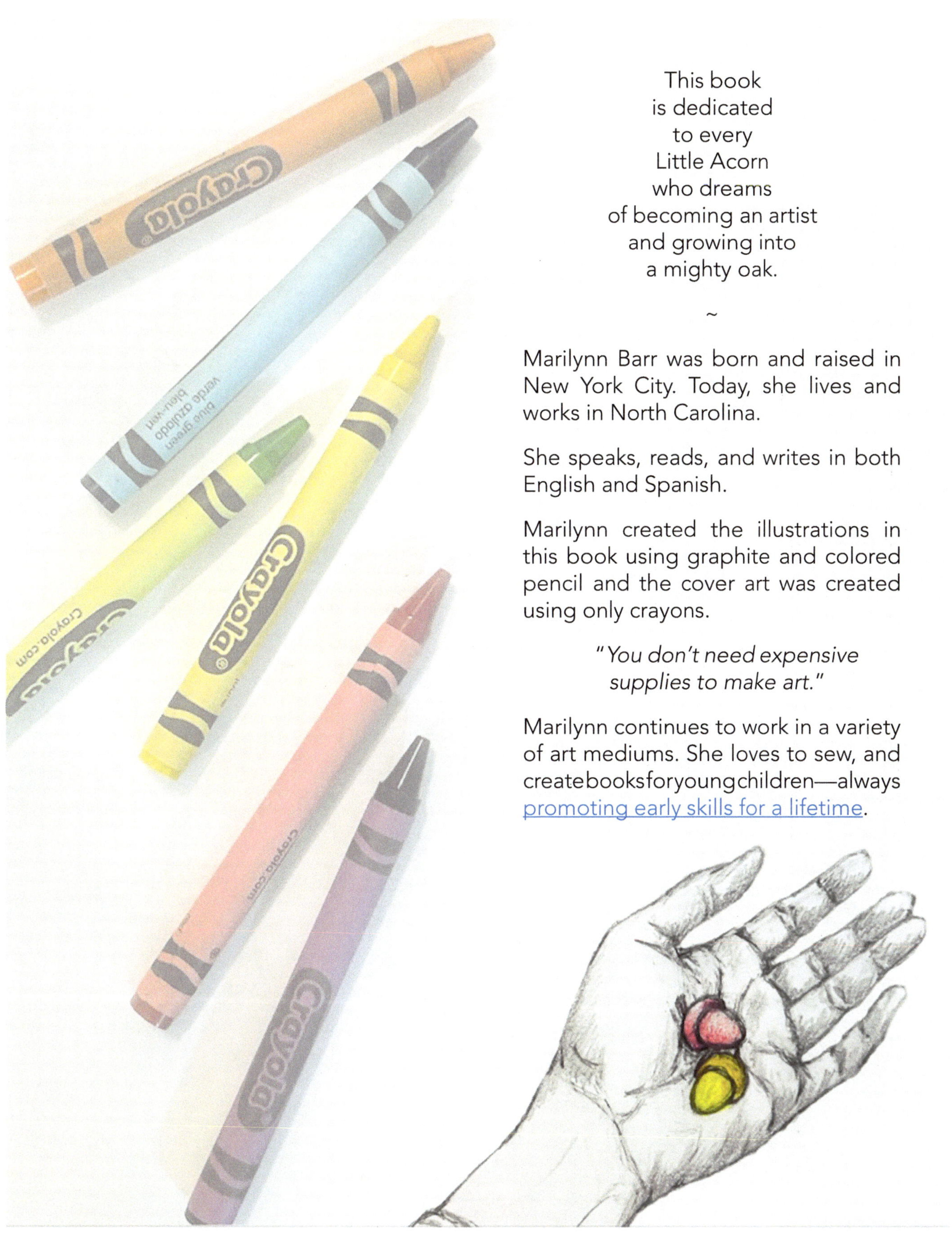

This book
is dedicated
to every
Little Acorn
who dreams
of becoming an artist
and growing into
a mighty oak.

~

Marilynn Barr was born and raised in New York City. Today, she lives and works in North Carolina.

She speaks, reads, and writes in both English and Spanish.

Marilynn created the illustrations in this book using graphite and colored pencil and the cover art was created using only crayons.

"You don't need expensive supplies to make art."

Marilynn continues to work in a variety of art mediums. She loves to sew, and create books for young children—always promoting early skills for a lifetime.

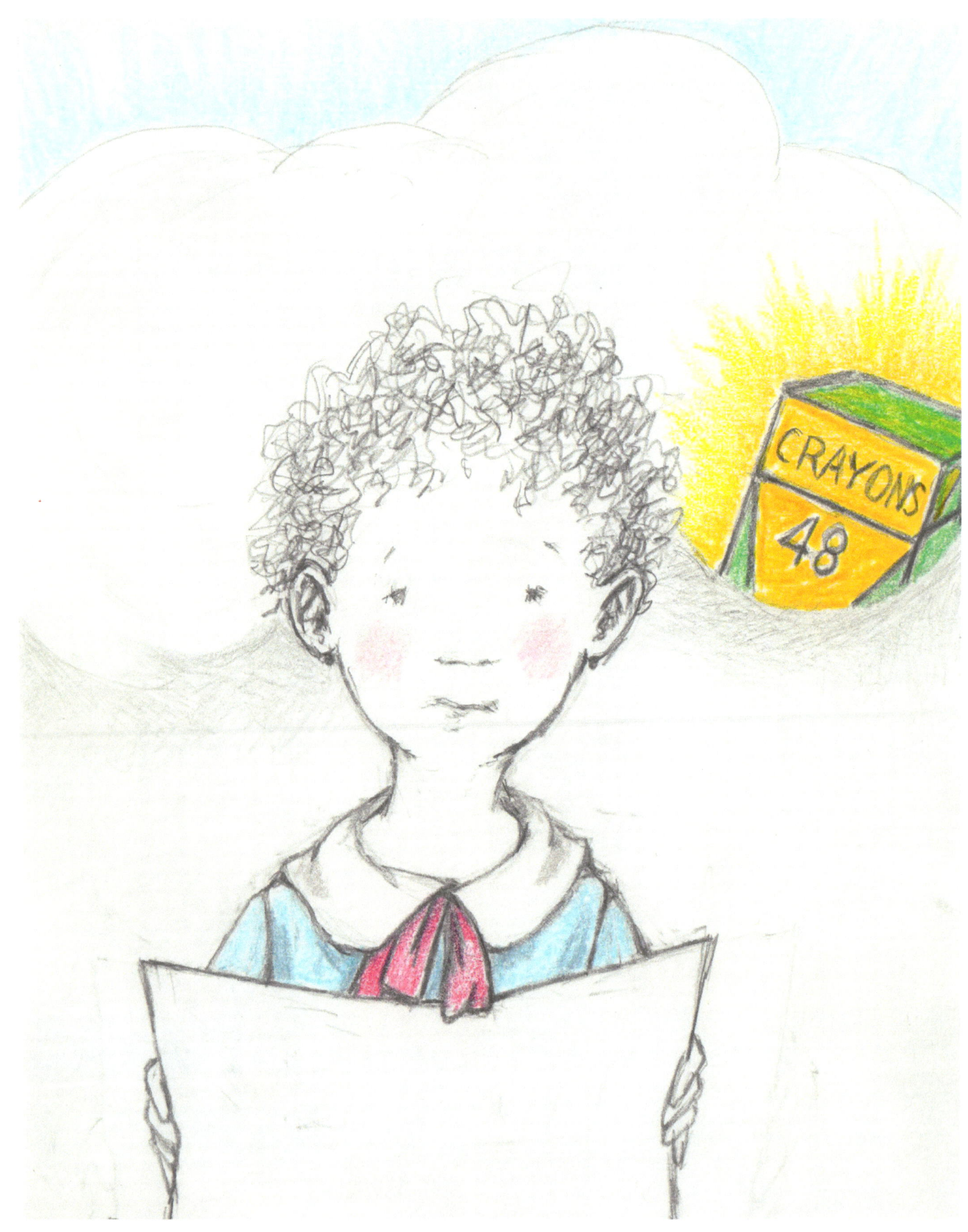
CRAYONS
48

Once there was a girl who loved to draw with crayons.

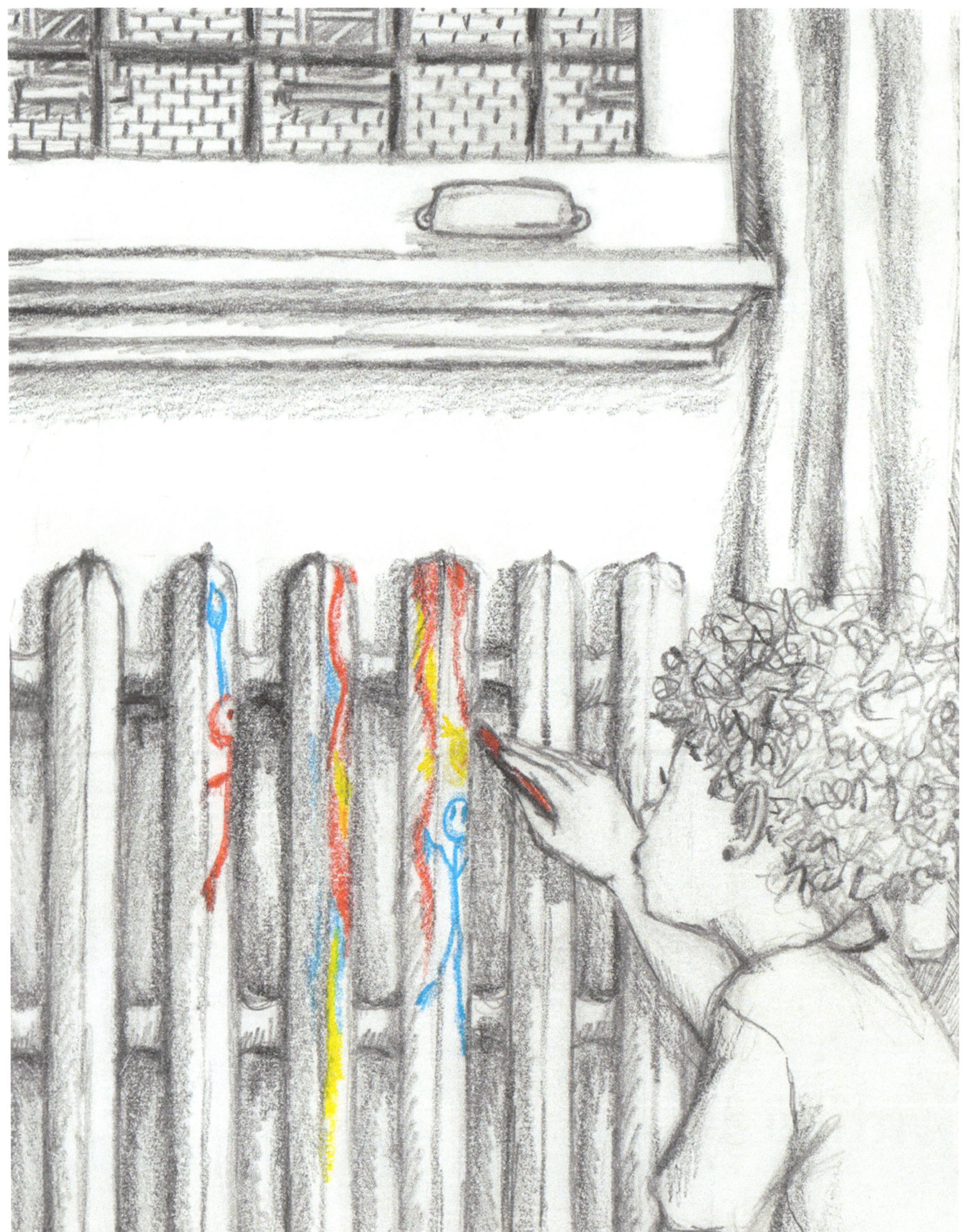

She drew on the radiator
when it was hot.
It made the crayons melt.
She soon learned that
that was a no-no.

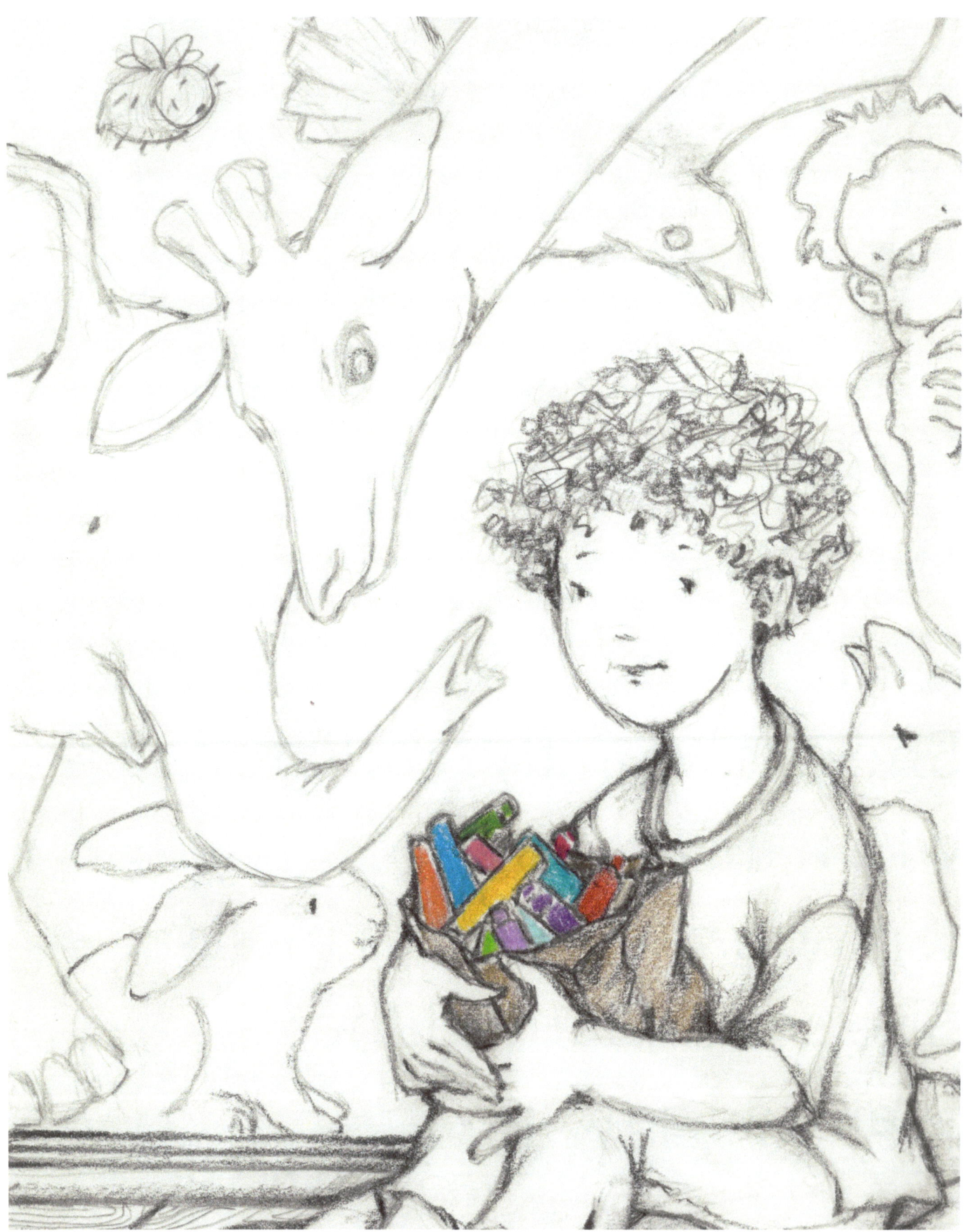

She imagined drawings
of all sorts of friendly animals.

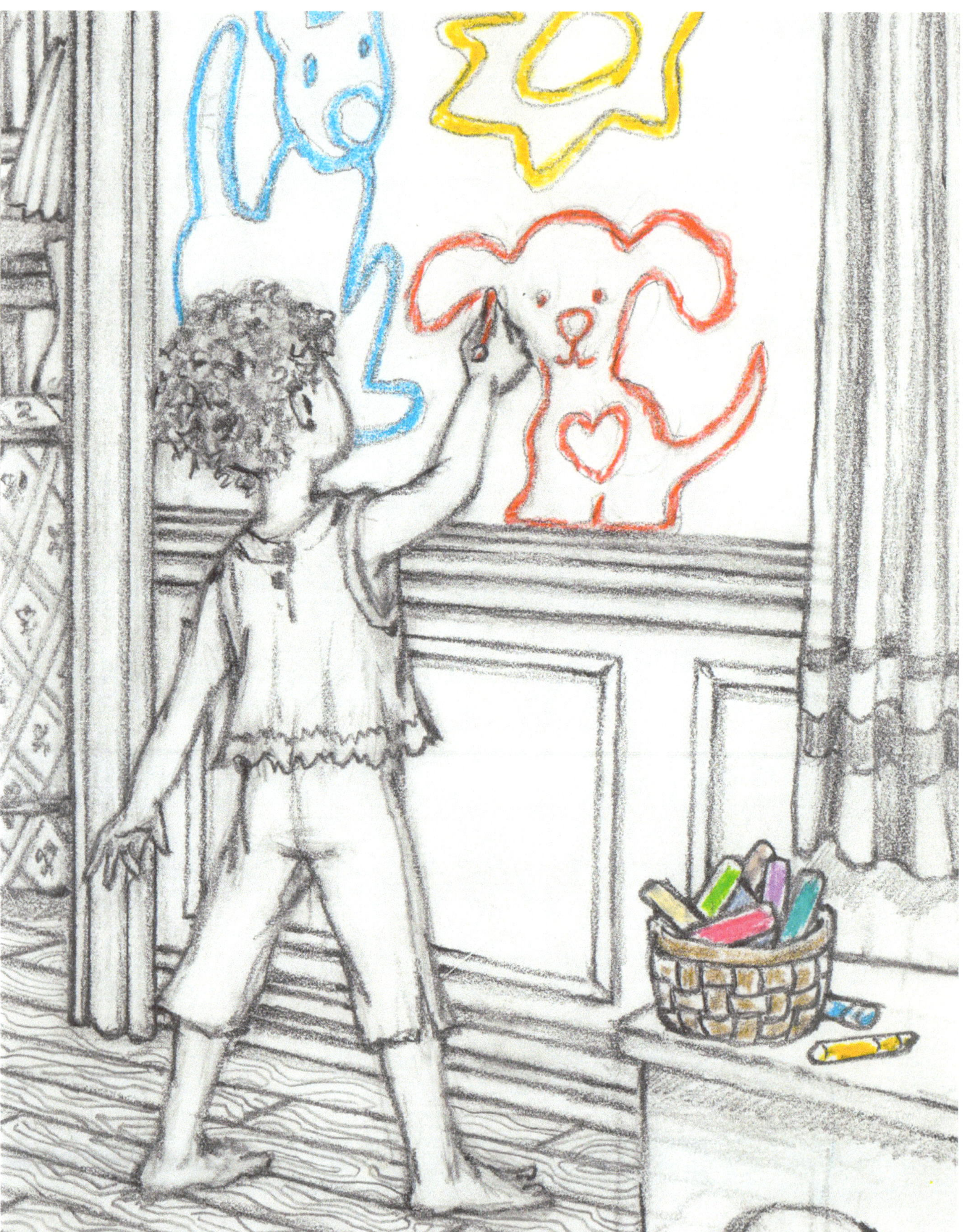

And drew some on the wall.
She learned that
that was a no-no too.

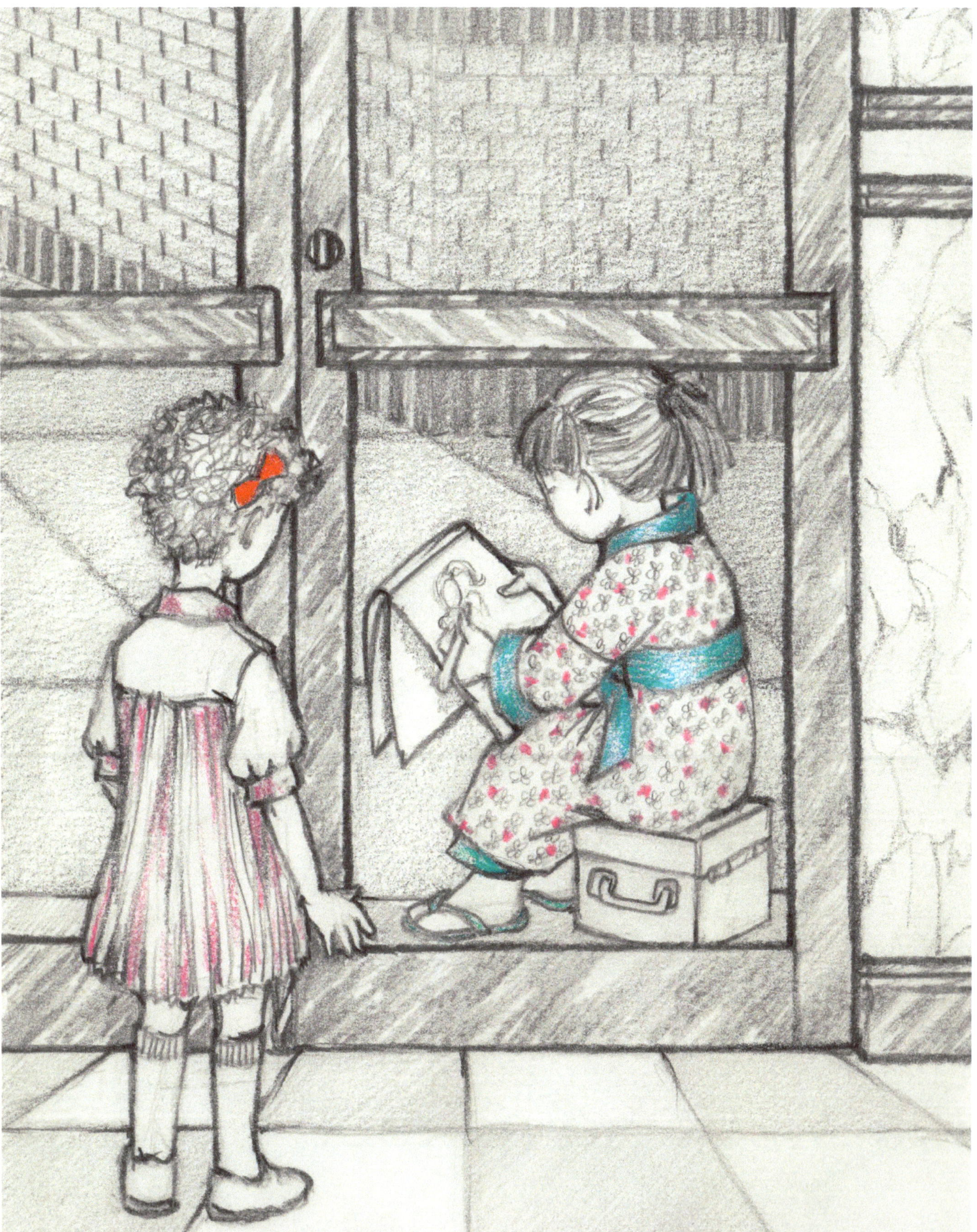

One day she discovered
a girl drawing in the courtyard
and thought,
"I want to draw like that."

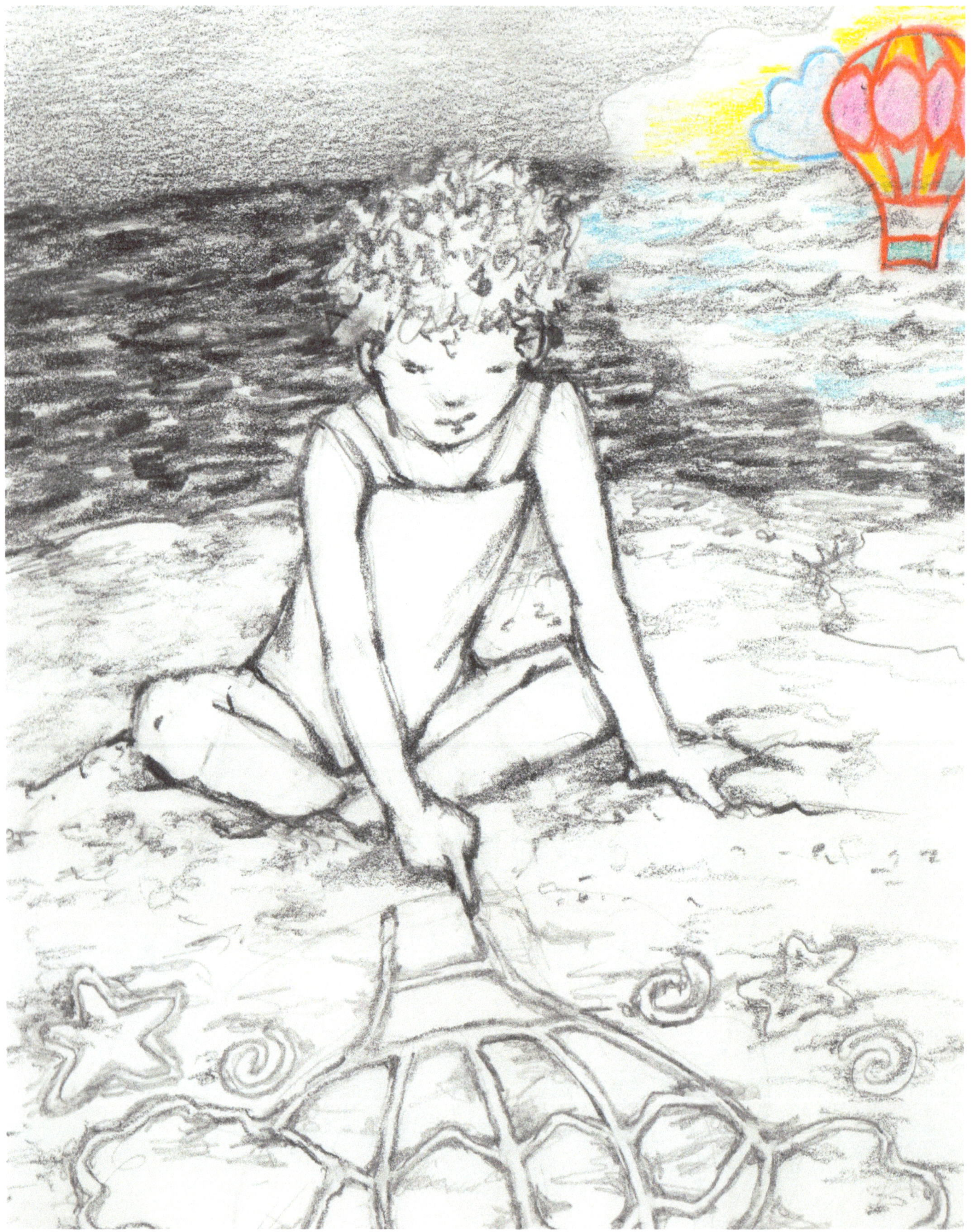

She drew with her crayons
almost everyday.
During the summer
she drew pictures in the sand.

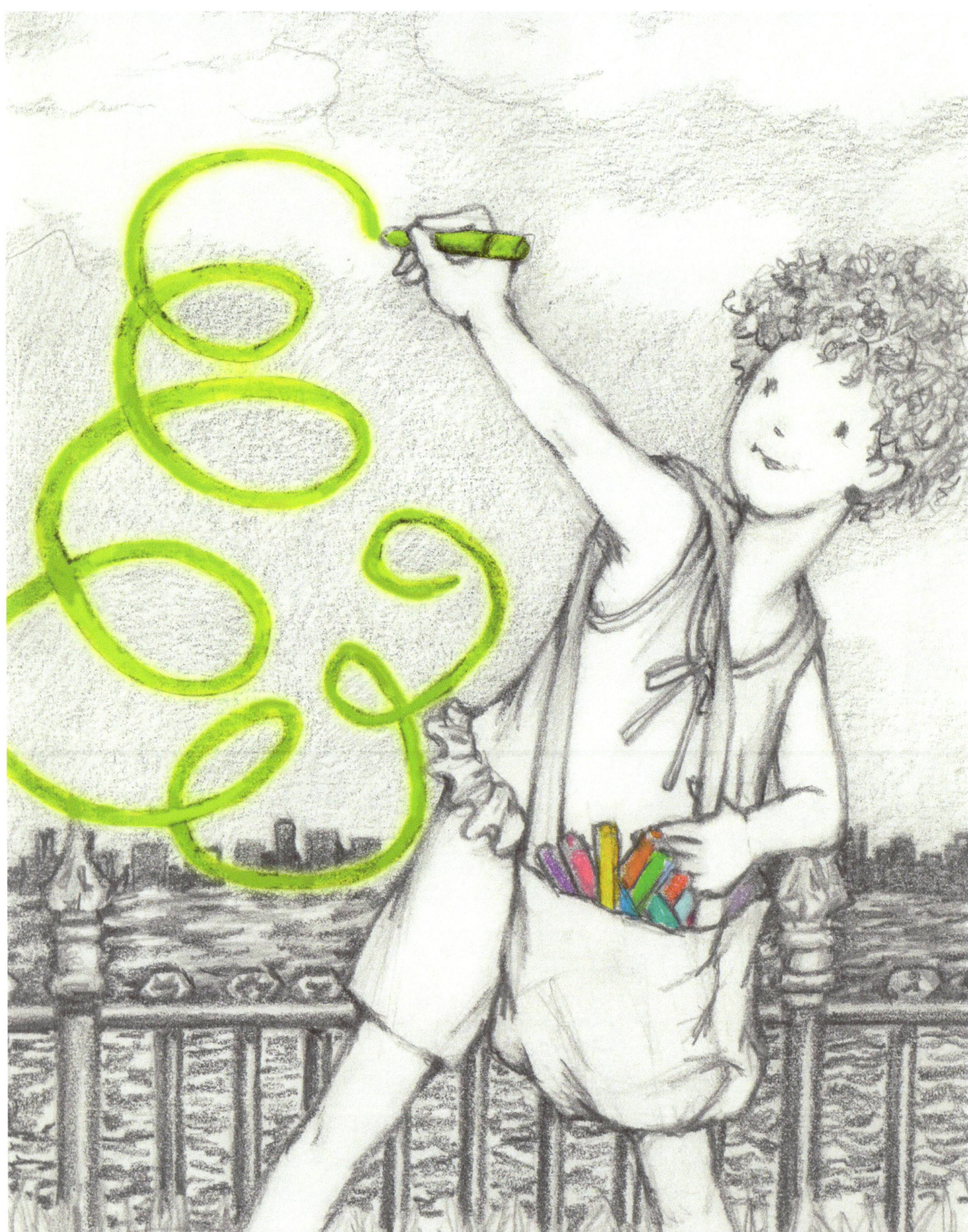

She carried her crayons everywhere and sometimes drew circles in the air.

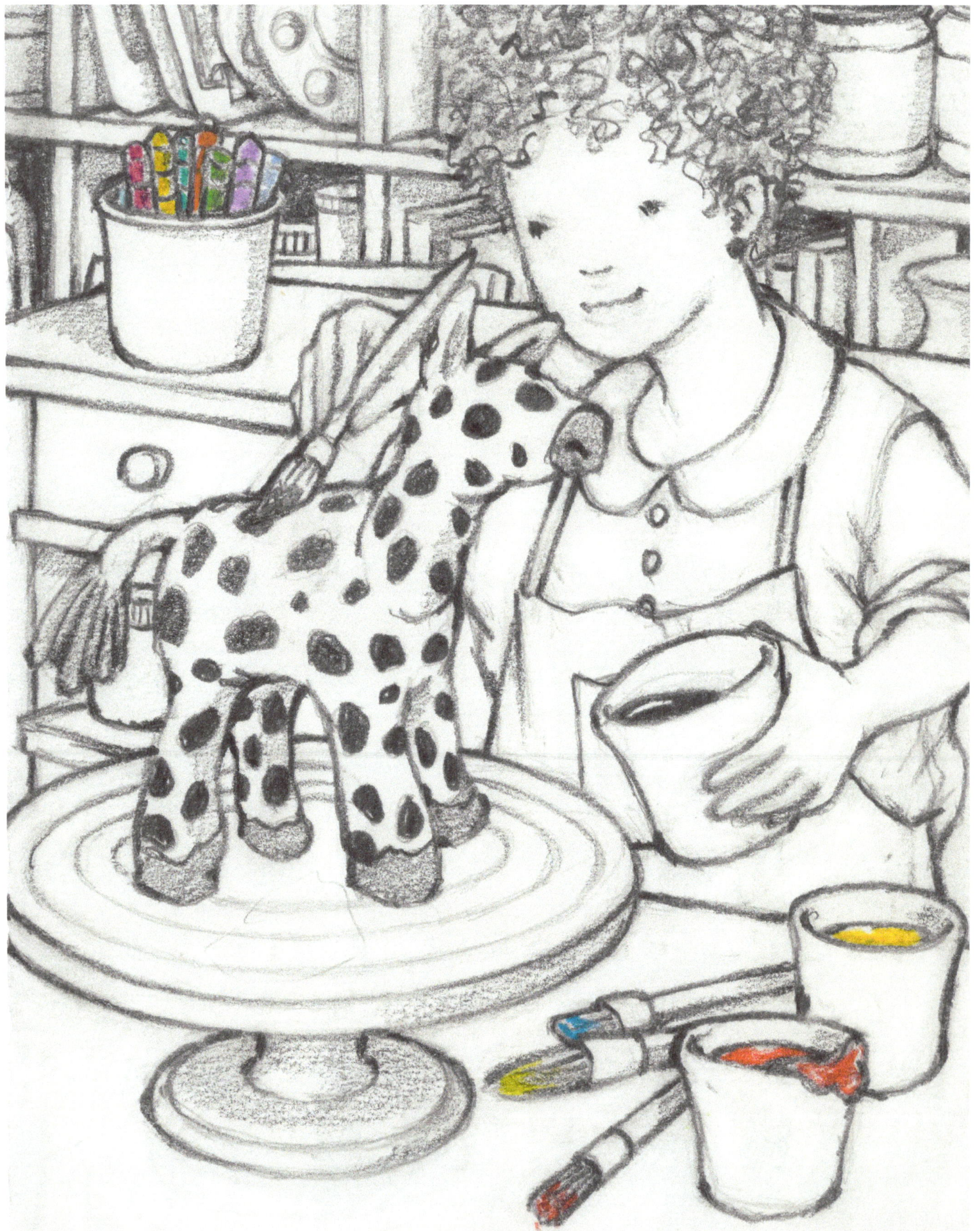

At camp, she made a polka-dot zebra out of clay.

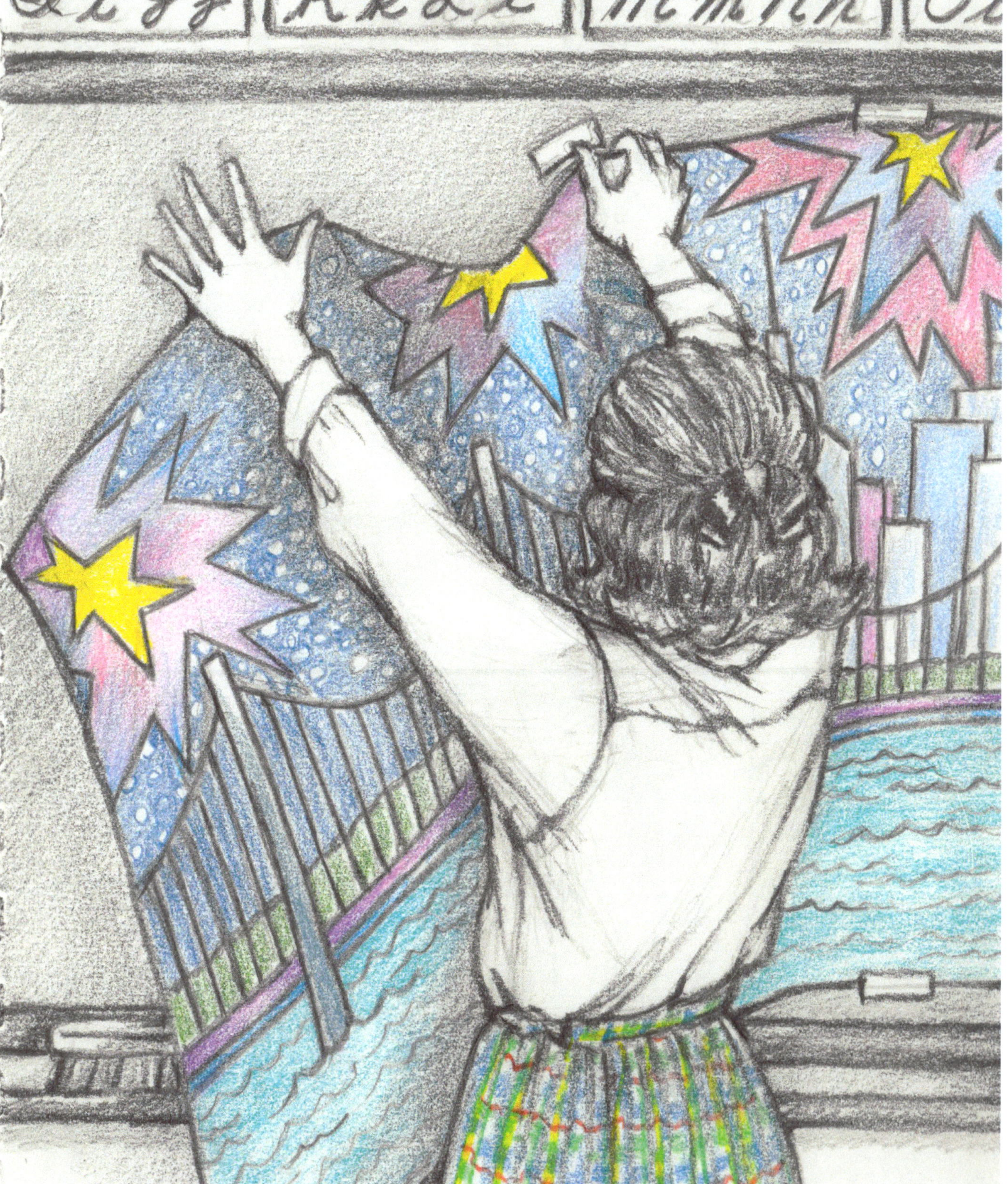
Ii Jj
Kk Ll
Mm Nn

When she grew a little older, she painted a mural of the city for her classroom.

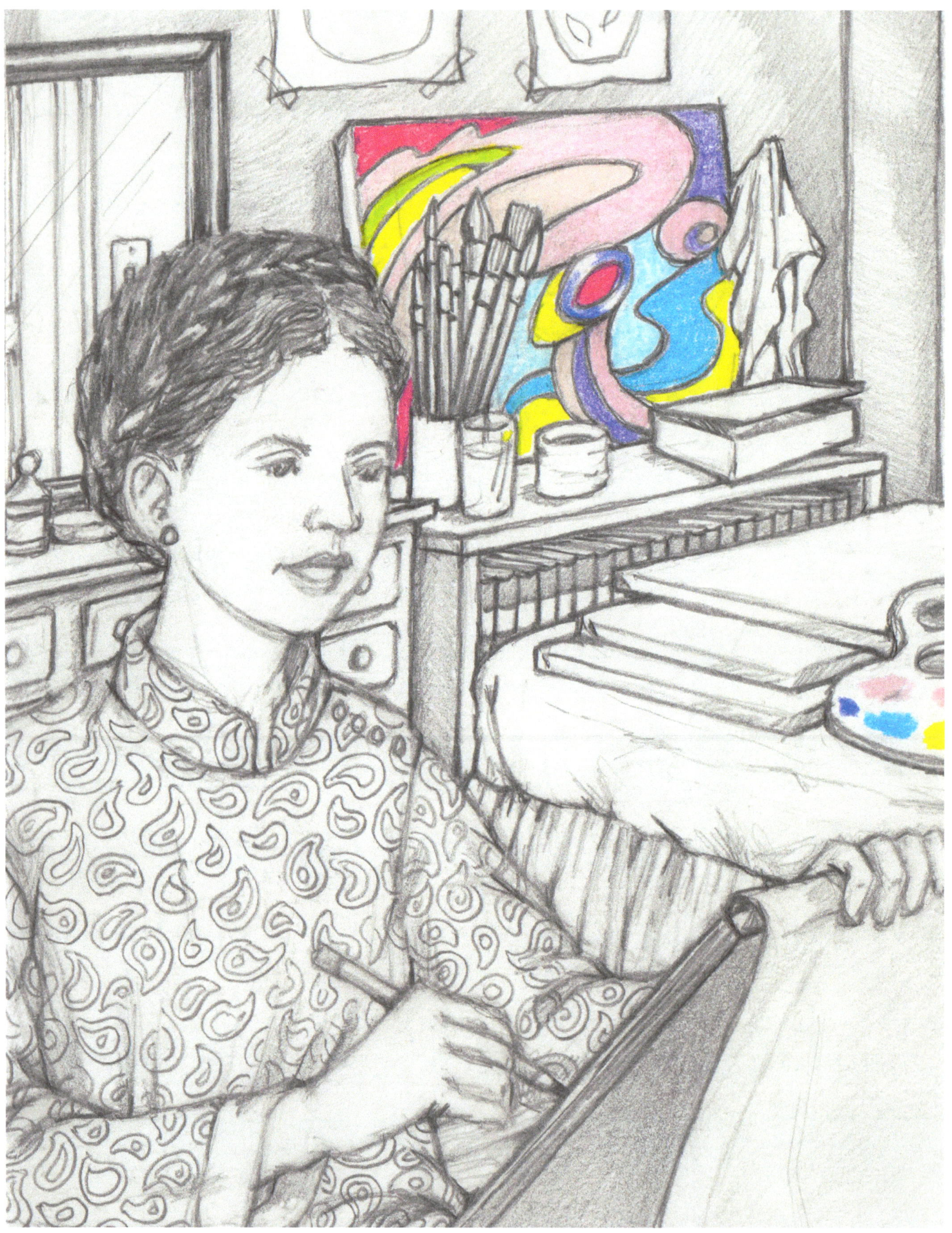

She practiced drawing
and painting in her bedroom.

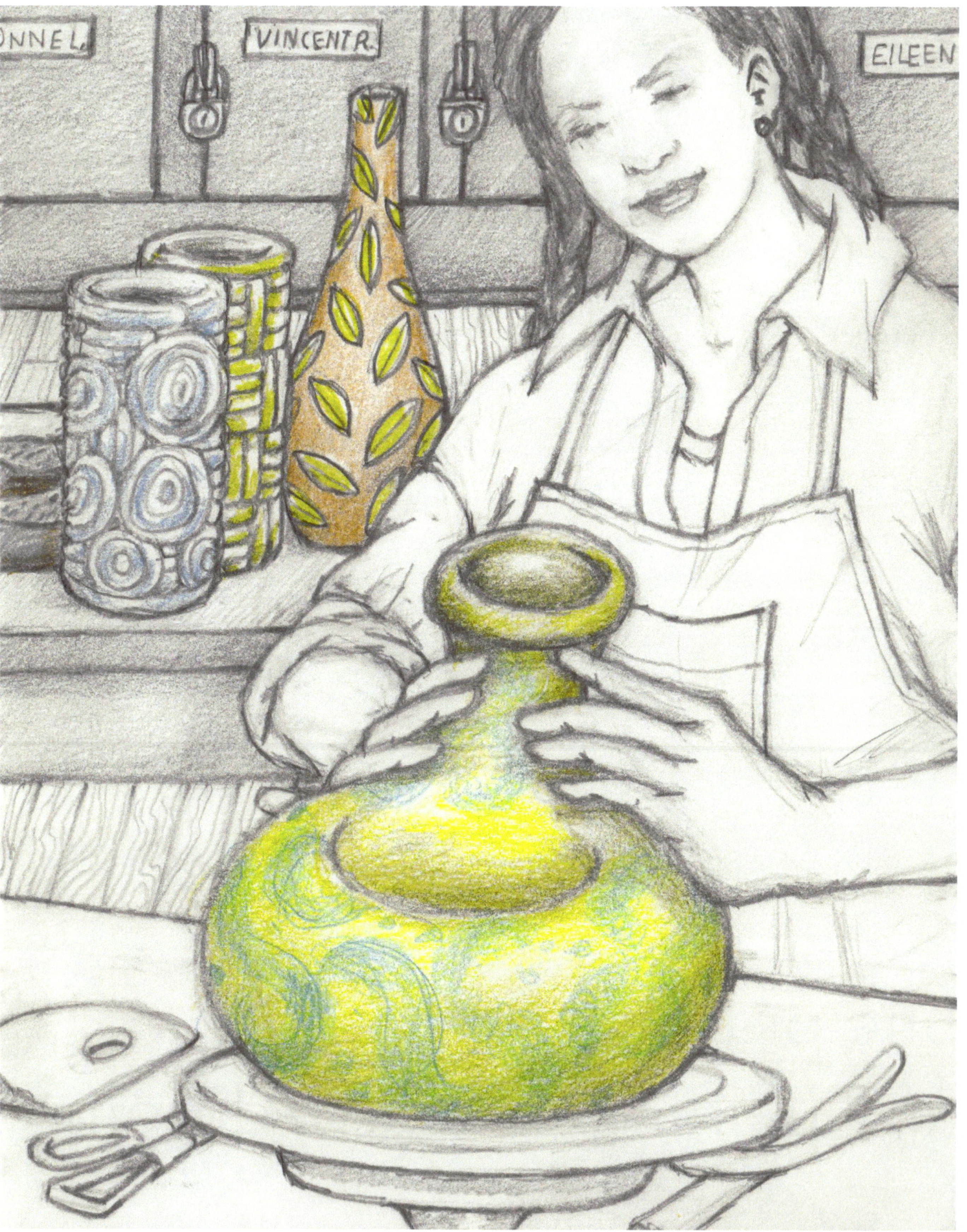
VINCENT R.
EILEEN

She learned to build vases
out of clay.

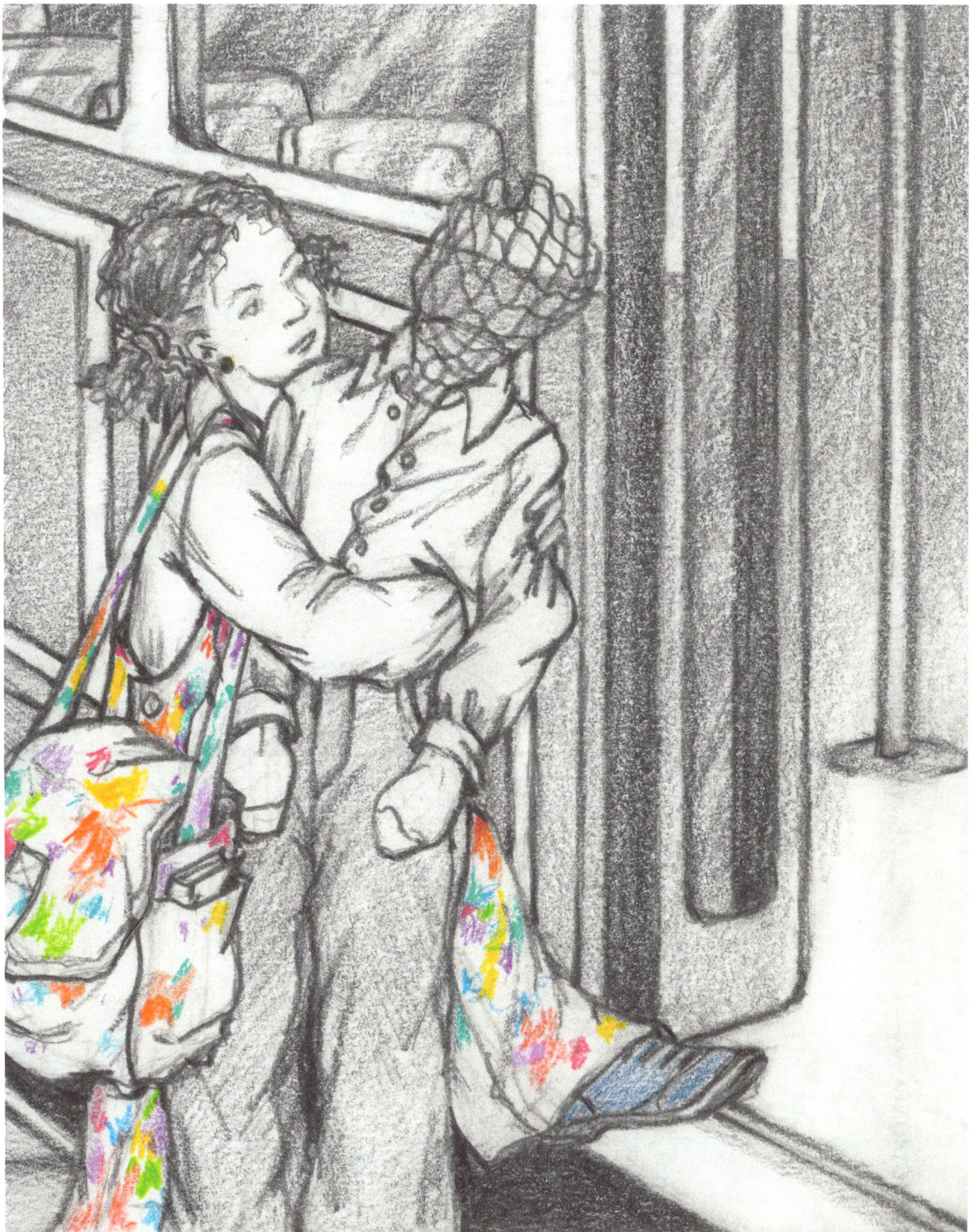

She even used
chicken wire to build
a life-sized mannequin
for a school project.

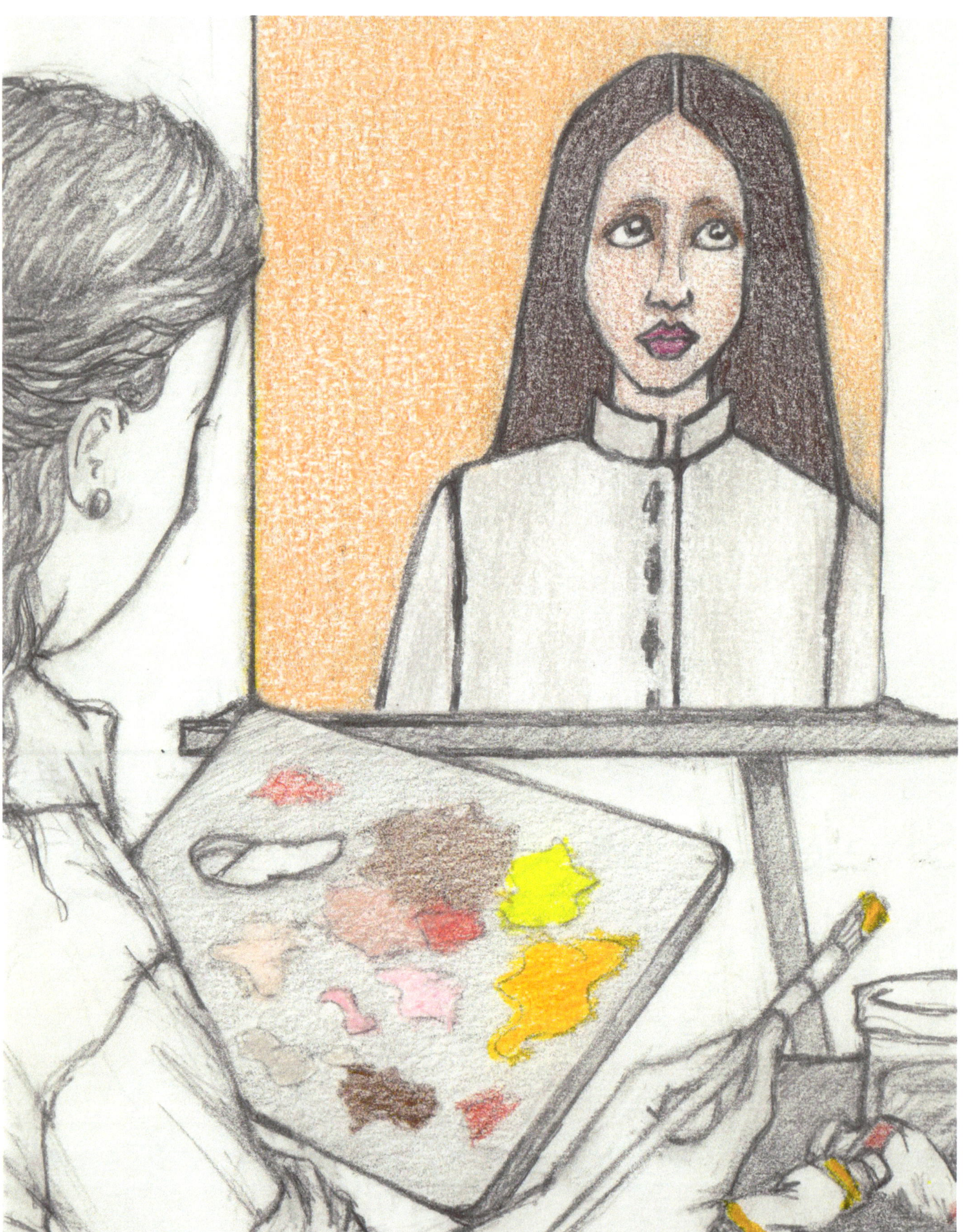

As she grew older,
she practiced painting
imaginary people.

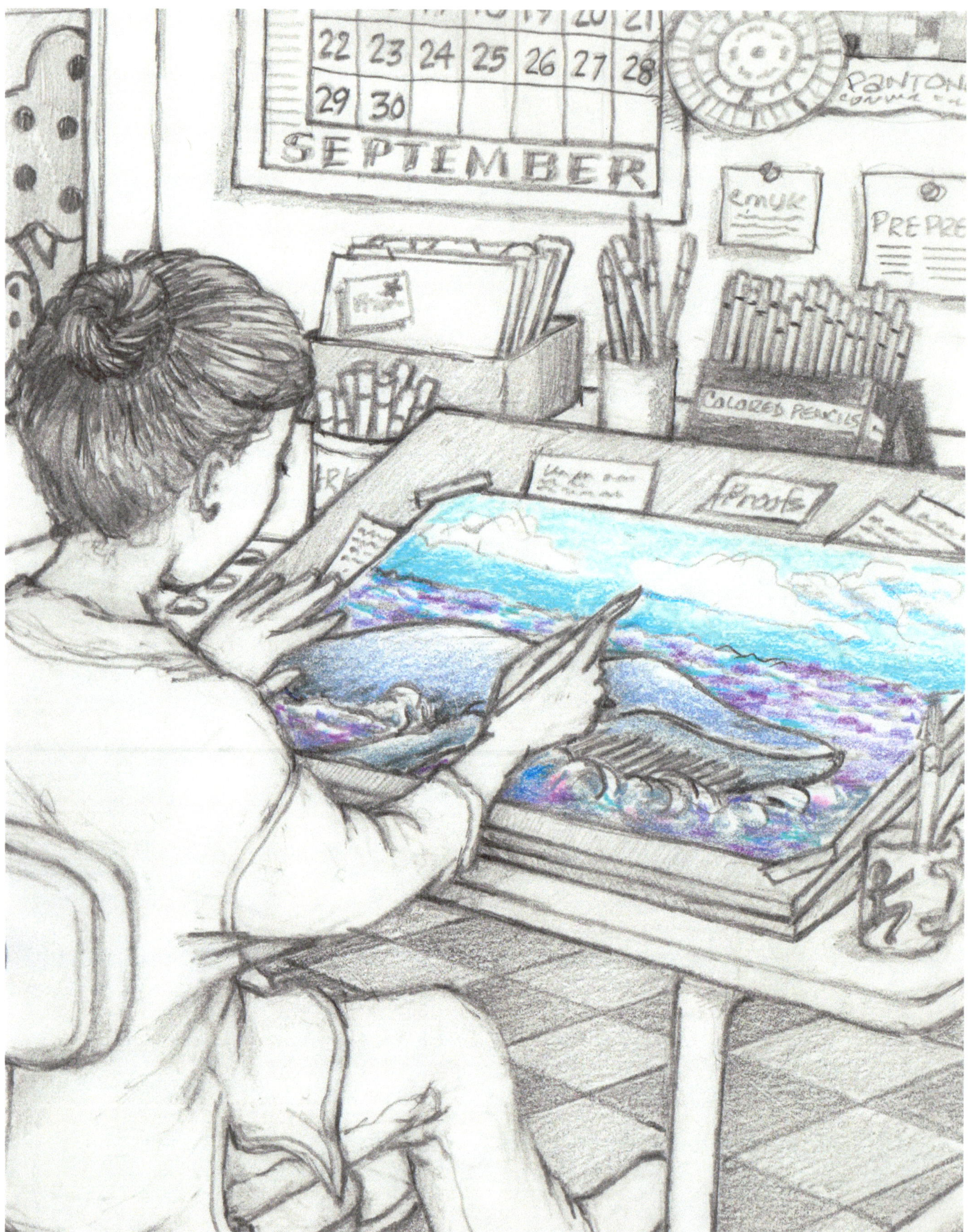

22 23 24 25 26 27 28
29 30
SEPTEMBER
cmyk
Proofs
COLORED PENCILS

When she was all grown up,
she got a job painting pictures
for books and magazines
of all sorts of things,
including whales.

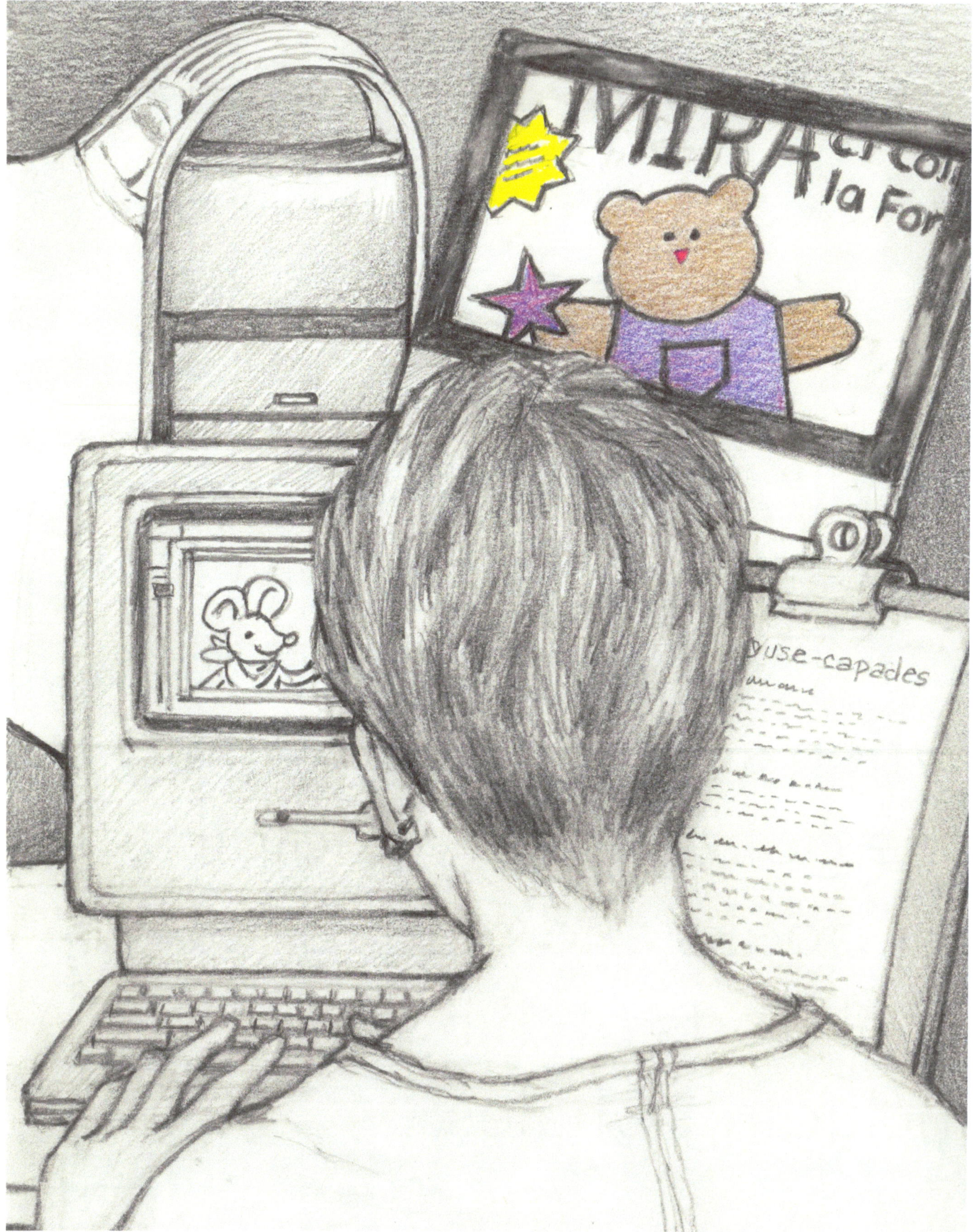
MIRA
la For
use-capades

She learned all about one of the first personal computers and used it to create books for young children.

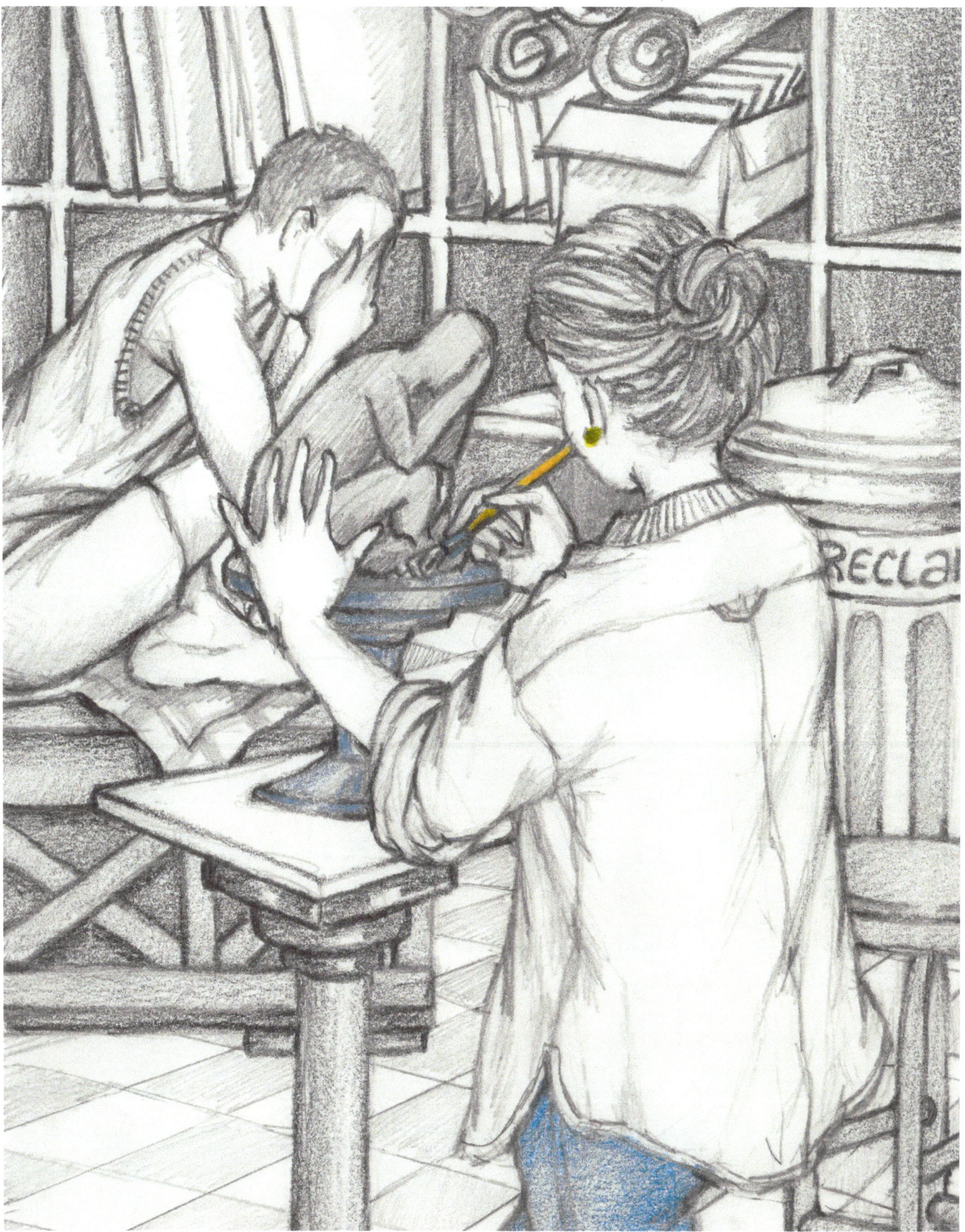
RECLA

When she wasn't working, she practiced sculpting figures out of clay.

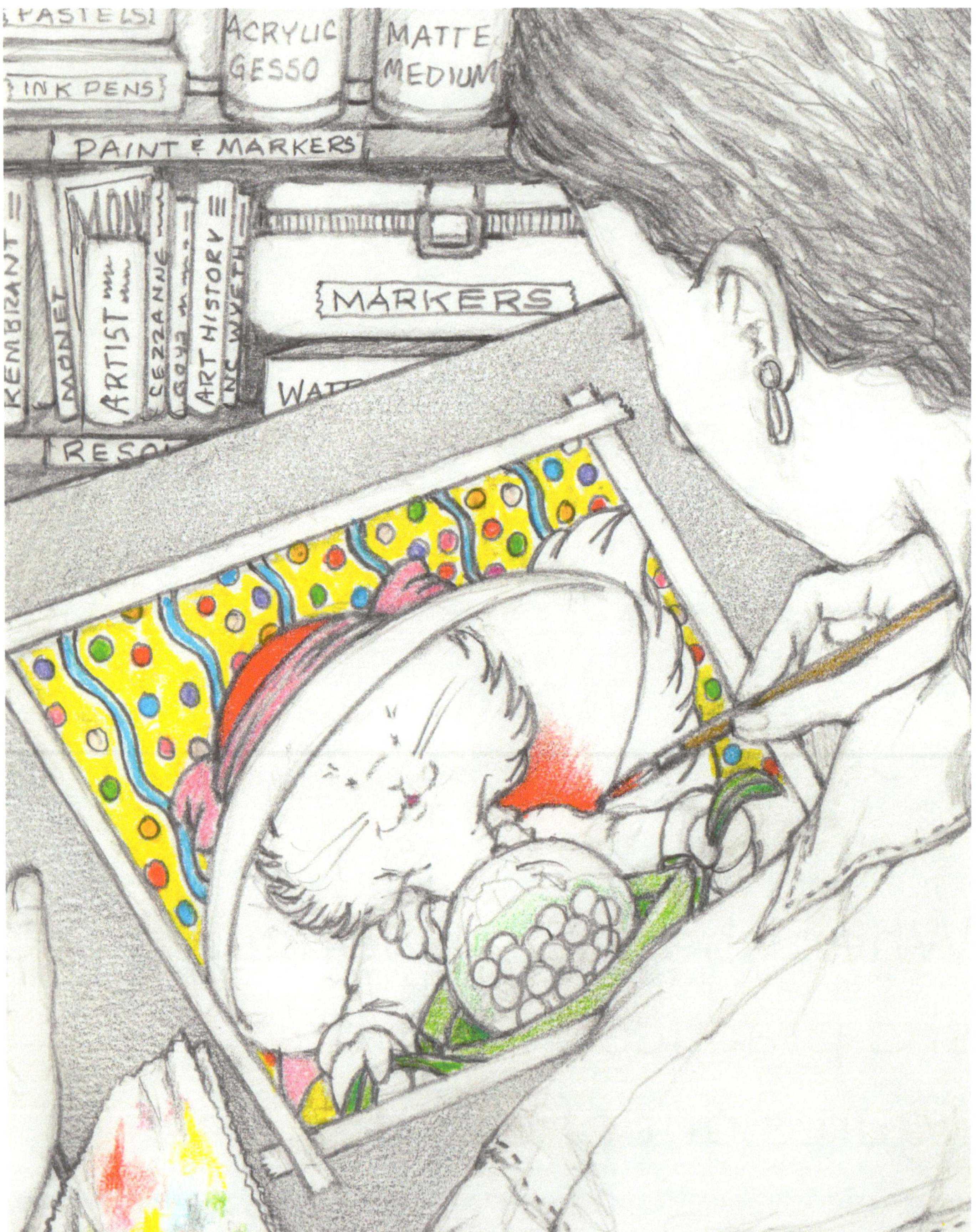

PASTELS
ACRYLIC GESSO
MATTE MEDIUM
INK PENS
PAINT & MARKERS
REMBRANT
MONET
ARTIST
CEZZANNE
GOYA
ART HISTORY
NC WYETH
MARKERS

She invented characters
for her first picture book
about a cat, and her friends.

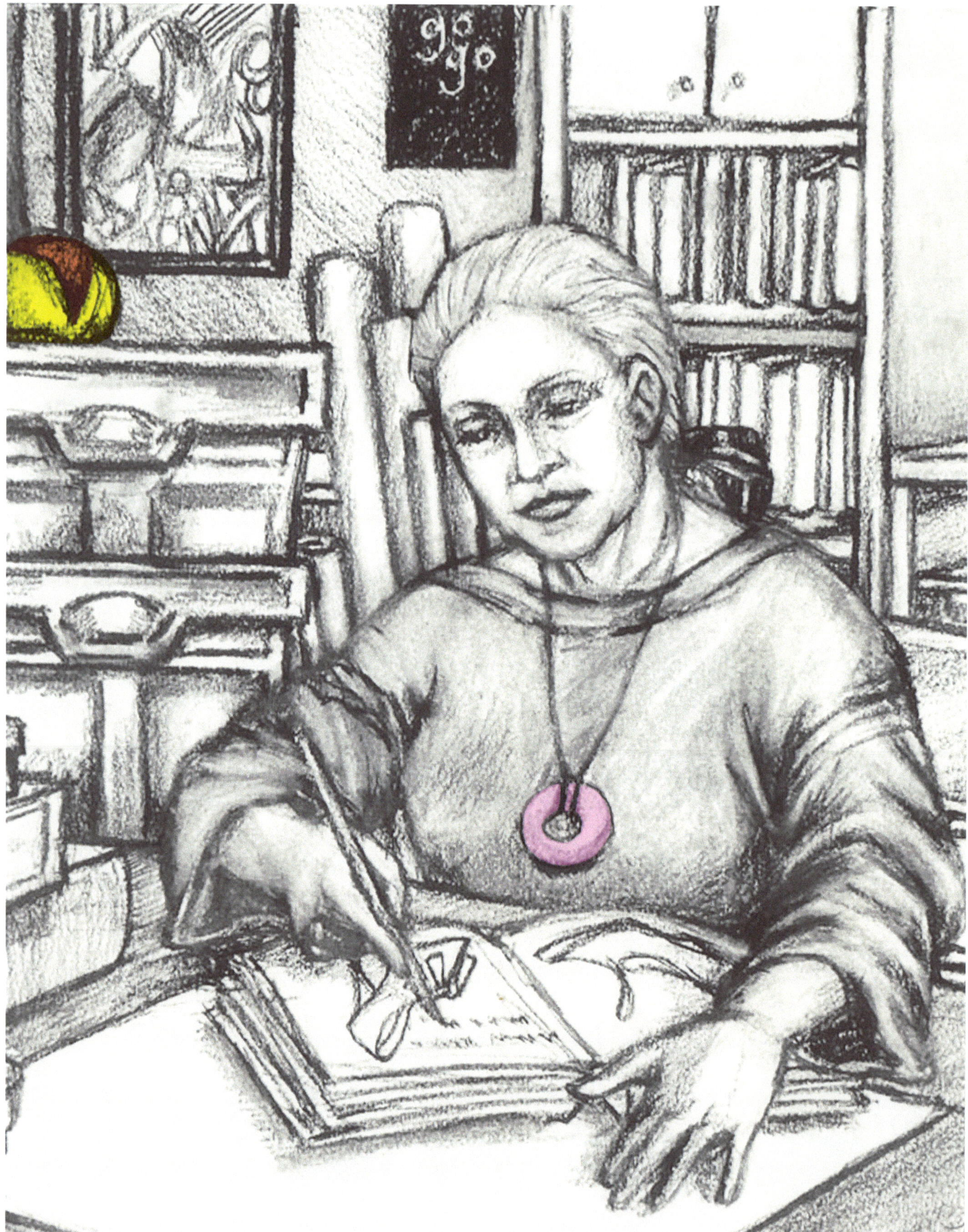

When she was much older, she began drawing sketches of shoes.

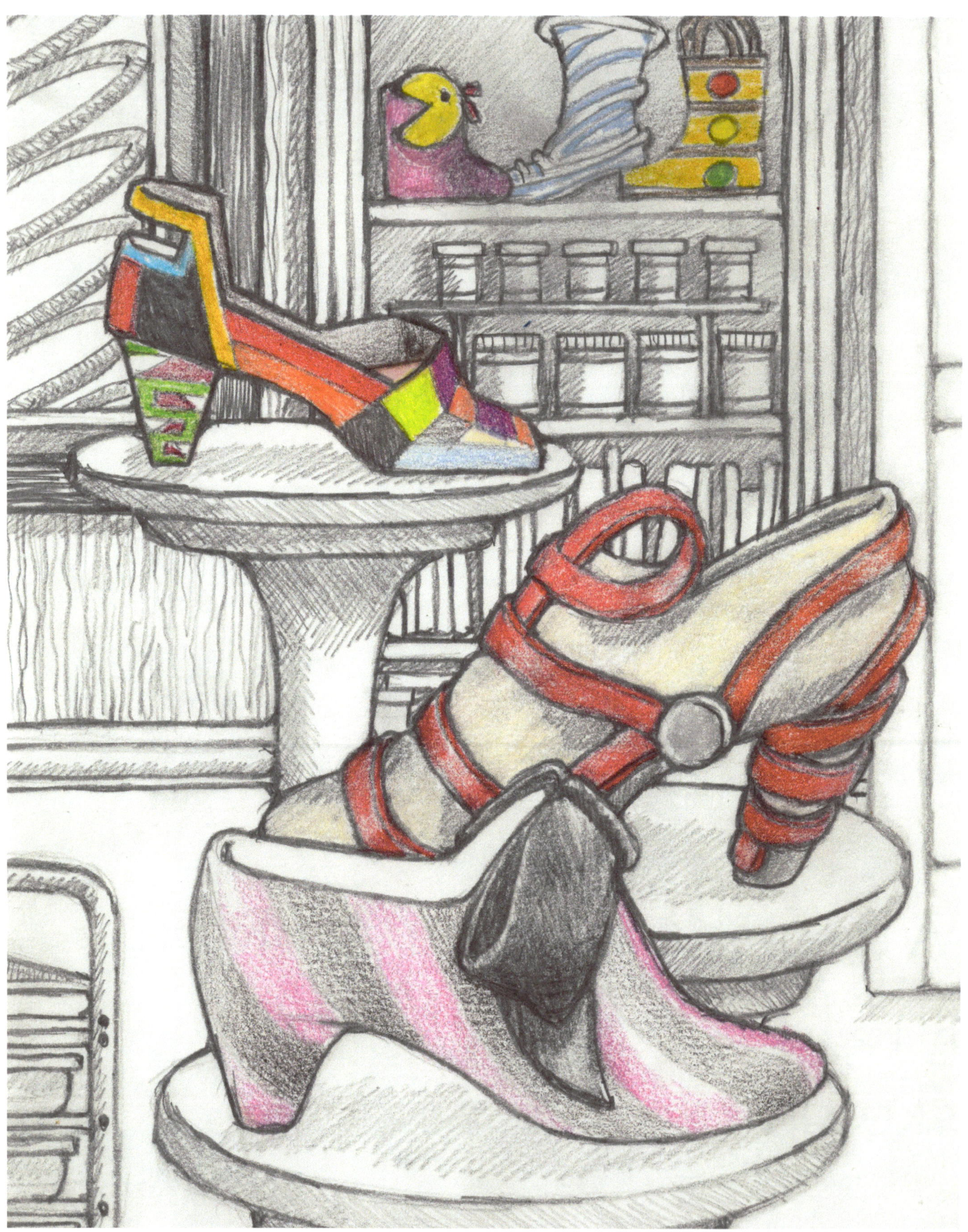

And turned them into a collection of clay sculptures.

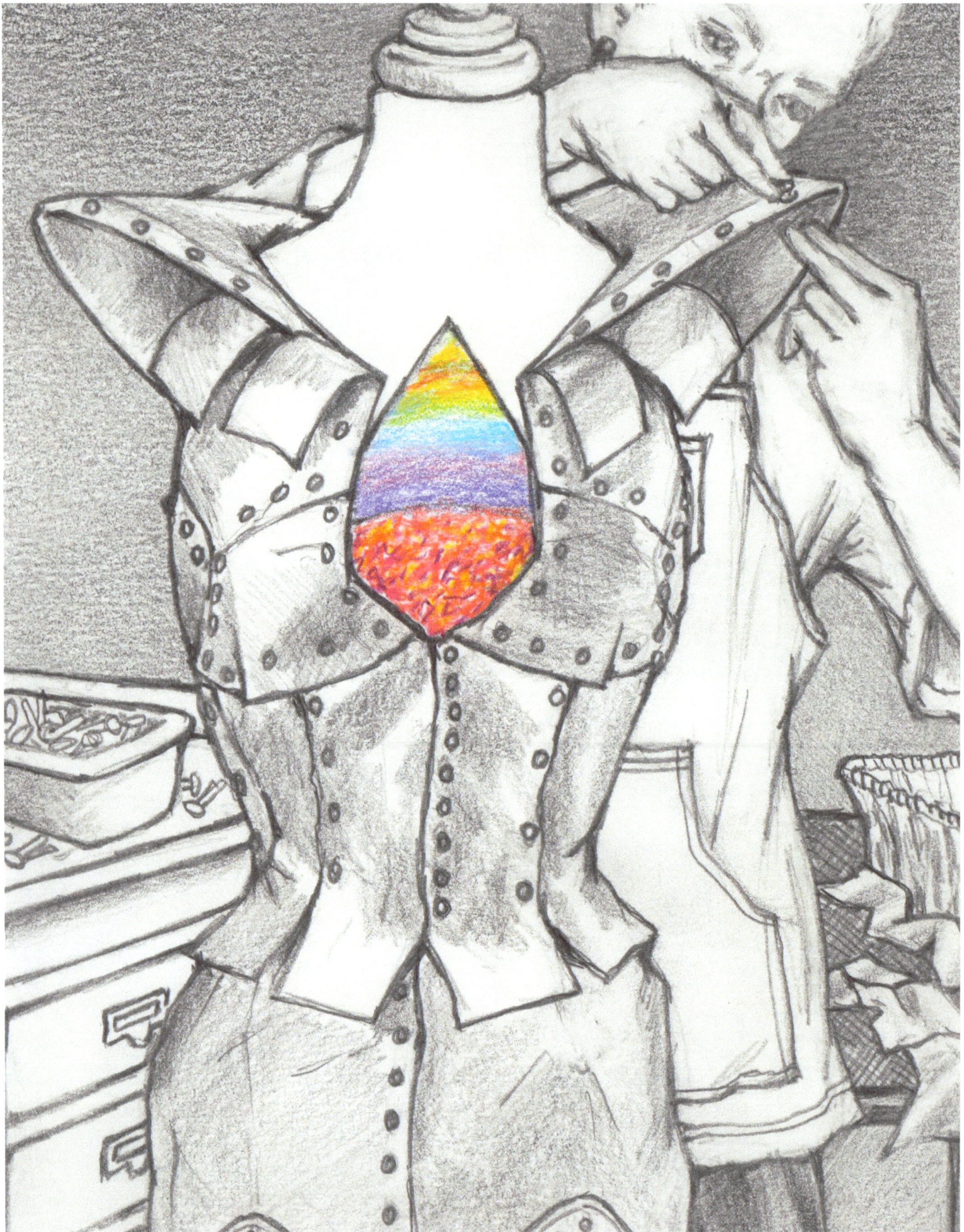

Her drawings, paintings, sculptures, and a dress she made from aluminum turkey pans and cookie sheets were included in art exhibits.

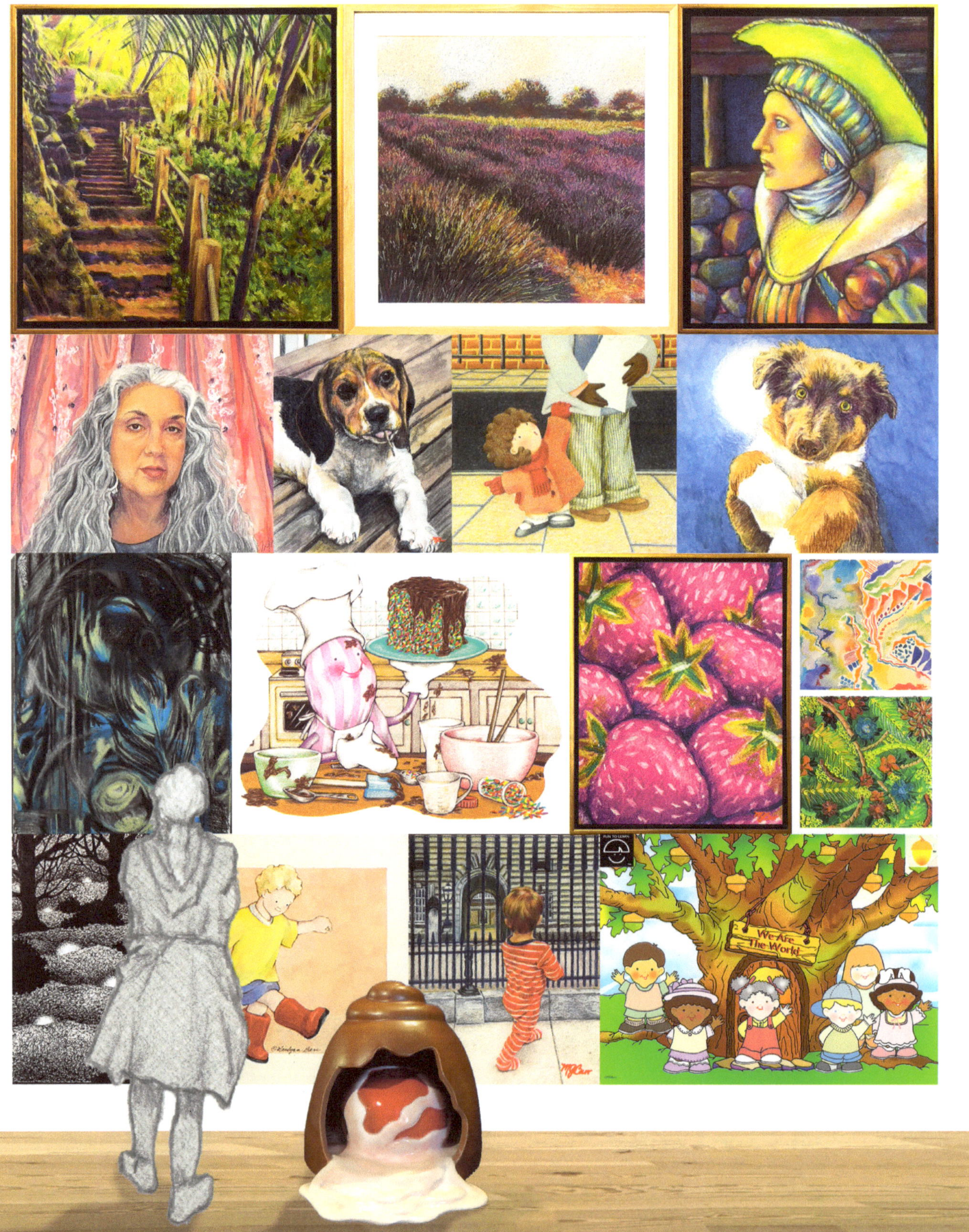
We Are The World

Today, she’s a grandmother
and continues to draw, paint,
work with clay, and
create books for children.

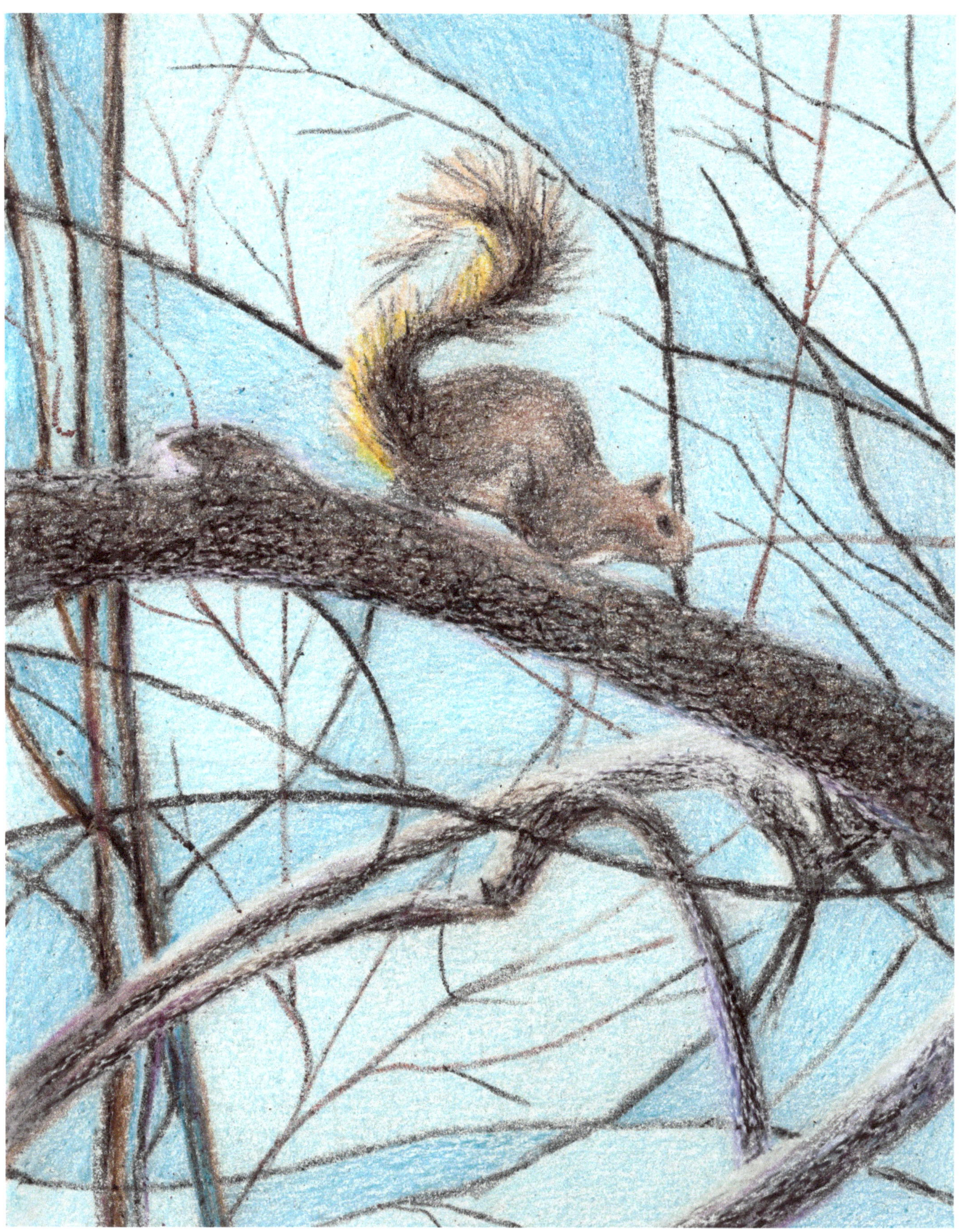

And she still loves
to make art
with crayons.

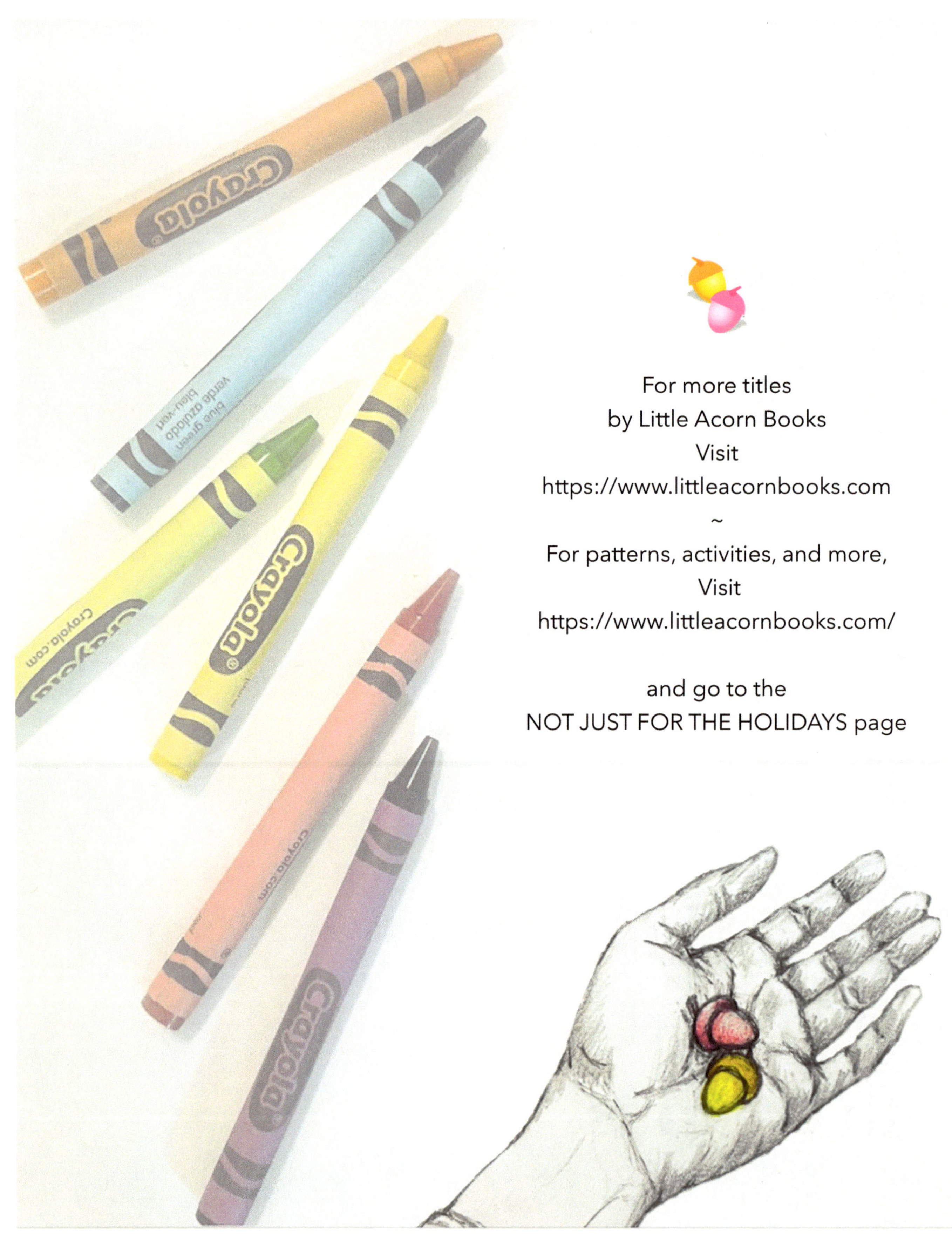

For more titles
by Little Acorn Books
Visit
https://www.littleacornbooks.com
~
For patterns, activities, and more,
Visit
https://www.littleacornbooks.com/

and go to the
NOT JUST FOR THE HOLIDAYS page

www.ingramcontent.com/pod-product-compliance
Lightning Source LLC
LaVergne TN
LVHW070154110826
845147LV00002B/395

* 9 7 8 1 9 4 6 5 5 7 0 6 3 *